Early Irish Communion Vessels

Michael Ryan

Country House, Dublin
in association with
The National Museum of Ireland

First published in 2000
by Town House and Country House Ltd.,
Trinity House, Charleston Rd
Ranelagh, Dublin 6
ISBN: 1-86059-090-X

In association with The National Museum of Ireland

Printed in Spain by Estudios Graficos ZURE

CONTENTS

EVOLUTION OF THE MASS

Origins

The Eucharist is the central act of Christian worship. It originated at the Last Supper when Jesus blessed bread and wine and gave them to his disciples. In most European languages, the celebration came to be called by a word (such as 'Mass' or 'messe') deriving from the Latin formula of dismissal at the end of the celebration – *Ite, missa est* 'Go, it is the dismissal'.

The early Christians had other ritual meals besides the Eucharist, but by the second century AD the distinctive characteristics of the Mass were codified. Prayers, thanksgiving, readings from scripture and blessing of the bread and wine mixed with water were described in a defence of Christian belief and practice addressed to the Emperor Antoninus Pius by Justin (martyred *c.* AD 165).

Gradually a distinction arose between the worshippers and the celebrant and his assistants. They were no longer partakers of a common meal but a congregation attending the ceremonies conducted by a presbyter (priest) who mostly faced away from the faithful. The table of the holy feast became the altar to which access was restricted.

Diversity in liturgies

The evolution of the Mass was not uniform throughout the early church. Different liturgies grew up around the great metropolitan churches of Antioch, Edessa, Alexandria and, later, Byzantium. In the west, there was a distinct Roman liturgy and a related family of 'Gallican' liturgies in the old Roman Empire north of the Alps. Spain, until the conquest by the Moors, had a liturgy of Gallican type called Mozarabic, which had strong Byzantine influences.

One reason for this liturgical diversity was linguistic. In the beginning, Greek was almost everywhere the language of the rituals but, as time went on, vernacular languages came to predominate: Latin in the west and other languages elsewhere, for example, Coptic in Egypt.

Photo 1 Ivory panel depicting celebration of the Mass. The altar is decked with fine cloths and flanked by a pair of candlesticks. On the altar are the chalice, a paten with heart-shaped eucharistic breads, the book for readings and, on the left, what may be the carrying case for the book. The ivory is set into the cover of a lectionary or book of readings for the celebration. It dates to AD 990–1000. (Liebighaus Museum Alterplastik, Frankfurt)

Elaboration of ritual

While the church was persecuted, the Mass tended to be simple in form and celebrated privately. The adoption of Christianity as a state religion in the fourth century, however, made possible a great sophistication of ritual. In the Imperial churches in Byzantium and elsewhere in the east, Mass was celebrated in imposing surroundings with elaborate prayers and music. In Rome, the liturgy remained at first comparatively austere although splendid churches were soon constructed. The collapse of the Empire broke up communications and led to some churches becoming isolated. North of the Alps, a varied pattern persisted with a wider permissible range of prayers and a number of other features which had gone out of fashion in Rome.

From the fourth century onwards, a number of popes began to reform the Roman liturgy and many western regional councils tried to promote conformity with Rome. The process of harmonisation was gradual, and minor variations still persisted into the later Middle Ages in places. The support of the King of the Franks (later Emperor) Charlemagne in the late eighth century was decisive in promoting uniformity in the west.

As liturgies became more elaborate and more complex, impressive architectural settings and furnishings were provided in wealthier communities. This process can be documented closely at Rome where the *Liber Pontificalis* (The Book of the Popes) records the magnificent embellishment of churches and the vast donations to them of precious vessels, furniture, pictures and silken cloth. Exceptional gifts of vessels and furniture were made in the reign of Pope Leo III (AD 795–816) by Charlemagne to mark his coronation as Emperor.

THE CHURCH IN IRELAND

Arrival of Christianity

Ireland received Christianity in the later fourth and fifth centuries from various sources. Slaves from Roman Britain – St Patrick, for example – may have been the first carriers of the new religion. Formal missions from Gaul and from Britain were organised. One mission – that of AD 431 led by Palladius – was a papal initiative. While it is probable that Palladius was acquainted with the latest liturgical practice in Rome, we do not know precisely what liturgies the earliest missionaries introduced but some were likely to have been variants of the Gallican family and, even then, might have been a little old-fashioned.

It is interesting that the Irish, uniquely in western Europe, did not use a word for the Mass derived from *missa*. Instead, they adopted the term *oifrend* (Old Irish) or *aifreann* (Modern Irish), which is derived from the Latin *offerenda*, a word occurring in a hymn chanted at the Offertory in the Ambrosian Rite of Milan.

Structure of the Irish church

The first missionaries seem to have founded a diocesan church with a regular government of bishops on the Roman pattern. Unlike the empire with its cities, towns, roads and central government, Irish society was fragmented and essentially rural. It was divided into many small kingdoms, although there were also some larger, powerful over-kingdoms. There were no towns.

It is argued that during the sixth century, monasticism flowered in Ireland and the great monasteries gradually took over the church: we now know that bishops and territorial dioceses, based on the small kingdoms or *tuatha*, remained important. Because of the varied origins of the Irish church, no clear metropolitan authority emerged for over four hundred years. This probably encouraged the survival of local variations in the liturgy.

An isolated church

Ireland seems to have been somewhat isolated for much of the sixth century. The changes that were taking place in Rome took time to disseminate, and so the Irish

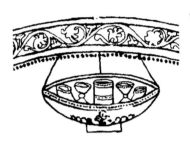

Fig 1 The Liber Pontificalis *(the Book of the Popes) describes magnificent donations of silver vessels to the churches of Rome. Many chalices were hung in the arches of churches as decoration. The original drawing of this hanging bowl containing sacred vessels, including two chalices, is in an arch of the canon tables in the bible of the Carolingian Emperor Charles the Bald (Bibliotheque Nationale Paris, MS Lat.1). It dates to the 9th century AD. (Drawing by C. Ryan)*

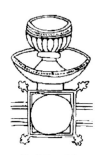

Fig 2 Detail from the Sacramentary of Marmoutiers, written at Tours about the year AD 850, showing a jewelled and fluted chalice within a large dish, also jewelled and probably intended to represent a paten. (A sacramentary is a manuscript containing all the necessary readings for the Mass throughout the year, with the exception of the scriptural passages.) This manuscript is preserved in the library of Autun in France. (Drawing by C. Ryan)

church fell behind current fashions.

When the Irish began to work as missionaries themselves in Britain and Gaul they must have appeared a little odd to Frankish and other colleagues who were in closer touch with current fashions. They were often accused of irregularities – the priest Egrestius, at the Council of Macon in Gaul in AD 624, accused the Irish of celebrating Mass with a 'multifarious variety of prayers and collects'.

The most celebrated irregularity was in the calculation of Easter – the Irish used an older method of computation and thus often celebrated the feast on different days from their Roman contemporaries. Conformity came slowly because of the fragmented organisation of the church in Ireland. The clergy of the south of Ireland, having sent a committee of enquiry to Rome, accepted the official Roman Easter in the 630s, but the northern Irish churches and the great monastery of Iona did not conform until the early eighth century. The issue was finally resolved in northern Britain, where Irish missionaries had been active, at the synod of Whitby in Yorkshire in AD 664. The meeting is described by the Venerable Bede as a dramatic set-piece confrontation between an isolated and backward Irish church that was defeated by the modernising and vigorous partisans of Rome.

The drama of that confrontation more than anything else has given force to the modern notion that there had been a distinct 'Celtic' church. Far too much has been made of this, especially by nineteenth-century clerics anxious to establish respectable historical pedigrees for national churches. When St Columbanus lectured Pope Gregory the Great in his letters, it was not as an aggressive schismatic but as a learned churchman who drew on valid, but older, traditions of western Christianity. To the seventh-century Roman bishop, he would have appeared more as a presumptuous provincial than a heretic. Irish liturgy, as recorded in eighth-century and later writings, like so much in the 'Celtic' church, was essentially Roman in character albeit with some superficial old-fashioned elements.

The Mass in early Ireland

We know quite a lot about how Mass was celebrated in early Ireland. The Stowe Missal, dating to about AD 800, gives the text of the Mass and the rubrics (directions to the celebrant, so-called because they were written in red). It also contains a treatise on the Mass in Old Irish, explaining the symbolism of each stage in the ritual and giving elaborate instructions for the breaking of the bread on special feast days.

We know that the chalice was prepared with watered wine before Mass began and brought veiled to the altar; it was uncovered in two stages during the liturgy. It is probable that the bread and wine were carried to the altar in solemn procession at the Offertory, although the Stowe Missal is silent on this point. Communion was received in the form of both bread and wine. In some cases we can be certain that the chalice was drunk from directly – the seventh-century monastic rule of St Columbanus prescribes a punishment for those who damage the chalice with their teeth. It is also possible that the people received communion by drawing the wine up through a metal tube, called a *fistula* or *calamus*, but no Irish example survives and the written evidence for it is confused. The fistula was widely used in early medieval Europe and until modern times the Pope customarily took the Eucharistic wine through a short golden tube on solemn occasions.

The Stowe treatise prescribes that the Eucharistic bread at Easter and at Christmas should be divided into sixty-five pieces and laid out on the paten (the plate or dish for the communion host) in the form of a wheeled cross. This indicates that a loaf rather than individual wafers was used in the area in which the Stowe Missal originated.

This complicated *fractio panis* (breaking of bread) has been thought to show influences from the Mozarabic liturgy. In that rite, the particles of bread are also laid out in the form of a cross, each part being invested with symbolism based on the life of Christ. The eastern churches practised elaborate fractions of bread and similar rituals were anciently common in the Gallican liturgies. In the early Irish church it seems that two priests customarily broke the bread but a celebrant of the rank of bishop might do so alone.

Another ancient survival may be the prayer in the Stowe Mass for the 'most pious Roman emperors and all the Roman armies'. Such a prayer had been irrelevant in western Europe for almost four hundred years, although it was still included in Greek rites. It just might be a contemporary note – with the coronation of

Fig 3 A ewer suspended in an arch, from a drawing framing canon tables in the bible of Charles the Bald (see caption to Fig 1).

9

Fig 4 Drawing of a mosaic showing the Byzantine Emperor Justinian, accompanied by members of his court, carrying a bowl, probably a form of paten, in procession. The mosaic is in the church of San Vitale in Ravenna and dates to about AD 547. (Pl 2 is a colour photograph of a companion mosaic from the same church.) (Drawing by C. Ryan)

Charlemagne in Rome in AD 800 there were once again two Roman emperors.

The Stowe Missal sheds little light on the setting within which Mass would have been said in a prosperous Irish church of the time. To reconstruct this we must turn to other sources and to archaeology.

There were very clear notions about what constituted proper equipment for the Mass. The word *menistir*, which derives from the Latin *ministerium* and means a service of plate, is used in many Irish texts to indicate a communion set. One early historic source states that a church without a proper set of altar vessels could not claim ecclesiastical status in law.

We know from the early eighth-century Irish Collection of Canons (church law) and from penitentials (tracts defining the punishments for transgressions) that altars were covered with linen cloths, that basins and towels were provided for the ritual washing and that deacons assisted at the celebrations. It is likely that altar furnishings were kept to a minimum. The earliest Roman traditions suggest that only the chalice, the paten, the book for the readings, and two candles were allowable on the altar.

Many surviving ancient Irish churches are small and people have been misled into thinking that tiny oratories were the norm. However, remains of stone churches of substantial size survive – many with the characteristic irregular masonry, lintelled doorway and some with the stone roof and barrel vault of the Irish style. Surviving stone churches are probably no earlier than the ninth century and most are later.

Historical texts also make it clear that larger churches that could have accommodated congregations of a hundred or more existed. Many of these were of wood or wattle, with thatched roofs. Some had plank floors.

One exceptional church, the cathedral at Clonmacnoise, was built in AD 909 by King Flann Sinna and Abbot Colmán. It was the recipient of many important gifts and may have acquired an imported elaborate altar frontal in the early eleventh century.

Cogitosus, writing his Life of St Brigit in the seventh century, described the church of Kildare. It had two entrances and a wooden screen, hung with paintings, separating the sanctuary and the body of the church. The gold and silver-decorated tombs of St Brigit and Bishop Conlaed flanked the altar: above them, jewelled crowns were suspended. While this description must be treated with some caution, it is clear that the great churches of early Ireland could provide an imposing setting for the liturgy. This setting was matched in the beauty of the surviving altar vessels.

Photo 2 Small (7.5cm high) gold travelling chalice with gold filigree and turquoise ornaments, found with a paten at Gourdon, Chalon-sur-Saone, France, and dating to the early 6th century. (Bibliotheque Nationale, Paris)

Fig 5 A small, rectangular gold and jewelled paten with an openwork foot found in a hoard with the chalice at Gourdon. (Drawing by R. Murphy, National Museum of Ireland (NMI))

11

EARLY IRISH COMMUNION VESSELS

EARLY CHALICES AND OTHER ALTAR VESSELS

We know of three hoards containing altar vessels and one isolated find of a chalice from early medieval Ireland.

The Ardagh hoard

The first of these to be discovered was the Ardagh hoard, found in Reerasta Rath, near the village of Ardagh, Co Limerick, in 1868. It contained a beautifully decorated silver chalice, now known as the Ardagh Chalice, a bronze example damaged during finding and four gilt-silver brooches, one probably of eighth-century, two of ninth-century and one of later ninth- or tenth-century dates.

The objects had been partly protected by a stone when found and may well have been concealed during a period of Viking activity in the area.

The Derrynaflan hoard

The Derrynaflan hoard, found in 1980 at the monastic site of Doire na bhFlann, Co Tipperary, contained a silver chalice, a fragmentary paten (now restored), a hoop

of silver, probably at one time attached to the paten as a foot, a bronze strainer and a bronze basin. They had been concealed in a pit covered by the basin. They were also probably hidden in the tenth century as the chalice, the latest object in the find to be made, had seen very little use.

In the eighth and early ninth centuries, Derrynaflan had been an important monastery which, at one stage, enjoyed the favour of the king of Cashel, Feidlimid mac Crimthann, who died in AD 847.

Other altar plate finds

A small silver chalice was found with a copper-alloy, footed paten on a crannog at Lough Kinale, Co Longford.

A bronze cup with a cast stem and a disc-shaped foot, found, it is thought, in the River Bann and now preserved in the Ulster Museum, Belfast, was probably also made as a chalice.

A copper plate traditionally associated with St Tighernan of Errew, Co Sligo, was long thought to have been an ancient paten, encased in metal plates to enshrine it. The object, known as the Mias Thighernain (dish of Tighernan), now in the collection of the National Museum of Ireland, has recently been shown to be a later medieval dish probably of a type commemorating St John the Baptist.

The Ardagh and Derrynaflan chalices

The Ardagh Chalice is 17.8cm high and 19.5cm in maximum diameter at the rim, excluding its handles. The Derrynaflan Chalice is 19.2cm high and 21cm in diameter. Both have paired handles at rim-level, springing from decorative escutcheons. A band of filigree ornaments passing through the handles girdles the bowl of each. Both chalices have hammered silver bowls, cast complex cylindrical stems, large decorated feet with a marked footring. Both carry lavish ornament on the underside. Both chalices use similar techniques of assembly: they are built up of more than three hundred components and the bowl, the stem and

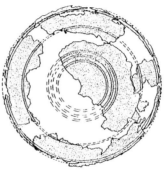

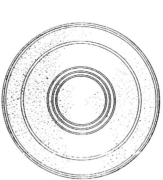

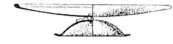

Photo 4 Small (height 6.05cm, diameter 11cm) copper-alloy chalice formerly in the Gracey Collection, Kilrea, Co Derry. Found, it is thought, in the River Bann. This vessel is similar in proportions to the copper-alloy vessel from the Ardagh hoard. Its foot is in the form of a disc with engraved ornament. It probably dates to about the 8th or 9th century AD. (Ulster Museum)

Fig 6 The small tinned, copper-alloy paten found with the little chalice at Lough Kinale. Fragments of this plate are shown above, and below is the reconstruction of the paten on its foot. (Drawing by Sadb Moddell, NMI)

Photo 5 The
Ardagh silver
chalice, side view,
showing the
ornament of the
handle, the bowl
girdle and the
engraved names
of the apostles
below the girdle.
(NMI)

the foot of each are held together by a stout bronze pin.

There are some contrasts. The Ardagh Chalice has a round moulding applied to its rim and, on the bowl, two round medallions containing crosses of arcs and filigree decoration. In addition, the bowl bears lightly engraved decoration, including a band with the names of the Apostles just below the girdle. The bowl of the Derrynaflan Chalice, on the other hand, is plain.

While the Ardagh Chalice has many ornaments of cast glass set like jewels, the Derrynaflan Chalice is enriched with amber. The Derrynaflan Chalice carries over eighty filigree ornaments, while the Ardagh Chalice has many fewer but of finer quality.

14

Photo 6
'Exploded' view
of the Ardagh
Chalice, showing
the main
components in
their correct
structural
relationship.
(British Museum)

15

Photo 7 Engraved ornament on the bowl of the Ardagh silver chalice, below one of the handle escutcheons. (NMI)

Some of the differences between the two vessels are important. The structure of the Ardagh Chalice as originally designed was unsound, and it had to be disassembled in ancient times and its hollow stem plugged with lead in an effort to stabilise it. The Derrynaflan Chalice, on the other hand, is structurally as strong today as it was when it was made.

16   *Cont. p 33*

Pl 1 Scene depicting the celebration of the Mass from the Golden Altar of San Ambrogio, Milan, about AD 850. Note that the top of the altar is bare of all but the essentials. Two deacons assist the celebrant. (Courtesy of M. Nava)

Pl 2 Mosaic showing the Byzantine Empress Theodora, accompanied by two ministers and seven of her ladies, carrying a chalice in processsion. The mosaic is in the church of San Vitale in Ravenna and dates to about AD 547. A companion mosaic shows her husband the Emperor Justinian (see Fig 4). (The Bridgeman Art Library)

*Pl 3 A hoard of
two chalices and
four silver-gilt
brooches, found
in 1868 in
Reerasta Rath (an
early medieval
ringfort) near
Ardagh, Co
Limerick. The
hoard may have
been hidden
during the
10th century.
(NMI)*

Pl 4 A hoard consisting of a silver chalice, composite paten, strainer and bronze basin found in 1980 in the monastic site of Derrynaflan, Co Tipperary. The objects may have been concealed during the 10th century. (NMI)

Pl 5 The silver ministerial chalice from the Ardagh hoard, decorated with gold filigree, engraving, cast gilt-bronze ornaments, glass, mica and amber. Probably dates to around the second half of the 8th century AD. (NMI)

Pl 6 The Derrynaflan and Ardagh chalices (NMI)

20

Pl 7 Underside decoration of the Ardagh and Derrynaflan chalices. (NMI)

Pl 8 The Derrynaflan Chalice, made of silver with gold filigree, cast gilt-bronze and amber ornaments. It probably dates to the earlier 9th century. (NMI)

Pl 9 Side view of the Derrynaflan Chalice, showing the handles and composite stem. Faint dimpling of the surface caused by hammering during manufacture may be seen. (NMI)

22

Pl 10 Ardagh Chalice, detail of the underside. Copper alloy disc decorated with cast ornament and gold filigree with a central rock crystal concealing the catchplate of the pin locking the assembly. (NMI)

Pl 11 Ardagh Chalice, detail of the polychrome glass and filigree ornaments of one of the handles. (NMI)

23

*Pl 12 Derrynaflan
Chalice showing
the gold filigree,
gilt-bronze and
amber ornament
of the stem
and footing.
(NMI)*

24

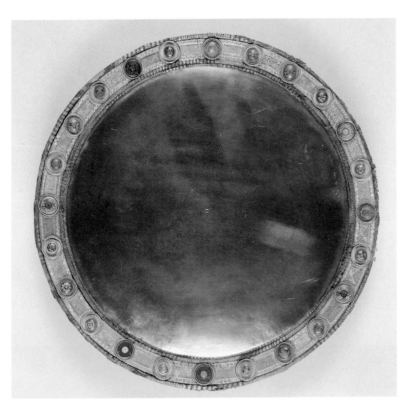

Pl 13 Derrynaflan Paten, viewed from above. It is made of hammered silver, cast gilt-bronze, knitted silver and copper wire with polychrome glass studs, gold filigree and stamped gold foil ornaments. It probably dates to the second half of the 8th century. (NMI)

Pl 14 Derrynaflan Paten reconstructed as mounted on its stand. The stand is decorated with cast bronze, stamped silver foil and polychrome glass ornaments. (NMI)

25

Pl 15 Side view of the Ardagh Chalice. (NMI)

Pl 16 Ardagh Chalice, detail of filigree panel showing a snake in the form of an interlace knot. (NMI)

26

Pl 17 Detail of the Derrynaflan Paten, showing in filigree, four interlaced serpents (left) and two backward-looking beasts (right). (NMI)

27

Pl 18 Detail of the Derrynaflan Paten, showing in filigree two kneeling men. (NMI)

Pl 18 Detail of the Derrynaflan Paten, showing in filigree two kneeling men. (NMI)

Pl 19 View of a handle and escutcheon of the Ardagh Chalice, showing the cast, polychrome glass, and filigree ornaments. (NMI)

28

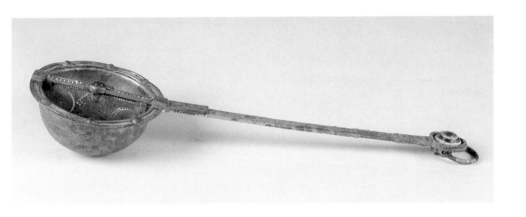

Pl 20 The Derrynaflan Strainer, made of bronze, with glass, rock-crystal and stamped foil ornaments. It is 37.8cm long and probably dates to the 8th century AD. (NMI)

Pl 21 A beautiful sieve, probably for wine, from the crannog of Moylarg, Co. Antrim. This exquisite pour-through strainer was found on what was probably a high-status secular site. (NMI)

29

Pl 22 Detail of rim and the top of the dividing plate of the Derrynaflan Strainer and showing the glass and silver ornaments. (NMI)

Pl 23 The Derrynaflan Basin, which covered and protected the other objects buried in the hoard. It is 44-46cm in diameter and dates to the 8th or 9th century AD. (NMI)

Pl 24 Bucket made of yew wood with bronze bindings, found in drainage of the Kinnegad river in County Meath during the 19th century. It is 14cm high. Small decorated buckets like this have both secular and ecclesiastical associations. They may have been used for serving wine or, in churches, for carrying holy water. Probably dates to the 9th century. (NMI)

31

Pl 25 Marble panel set in the wall of the Basilica of San Marco (St Mark's) in Venice, depicting two peacocks (symbols of the resurrection as their flesh was thought to be incorruptible), flanking a vase from which grows a Tree of Life. The panel was probably part of a screen in an ancient church in Byzantium, looted in the 13th century. (Author)

Pl 26 As Pl 25, showing two winged griffins flanking the Tree of Life. (Author)

32

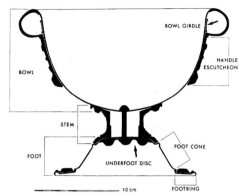

Fig 7 Composite structure of the Derrynaflan Chalice, as deduced from X-rays and surface inspection. (Drawing by Ursula Mattenberger, NMI)

Photo 8 Detail of the Ardagh silver chalice, showing a filigree panel of interlaced birds with glass studs at either end. (NMI)

Photo 9 Detail of the Ardagh silver chalice, showing a panel with plain interlace. (NMI)

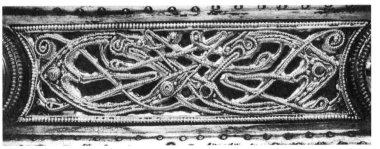

Photo 10 Detail of the Ardagh silver chalice, showing a panel with contorted interlaced beasts. (NMI)

33

Photo 11 Detail (inverted) of glass and filigree ornament of a handle escutcheon on the Ardagh silver chalice. The semicircular panel and the two axe-shaped panels depict interlaced serpents. (NMI)

Photo 12 Detail of filigree panel on the stem of the Derrynaflan Chalice, showing a crudely depicted bird with out-stretched wings. (NMI)

The Ardagh Chalice is more colourful and more refined, while the Derrynaflan Chalice relies on the lavish use of valuable materials to achieve an effect that is less striking. This suggests that they were made at different times, a conclusion that is confirmed by the close resemblance of the art of the Derrynaflan Chalice to some large brooches of ninth-century date. It is likely on similar comparisons that the Ardagh Chalice was made during the eighth century.

34   The filigree of the Ardagh Chalice is of exceptional quality – the wires are used to

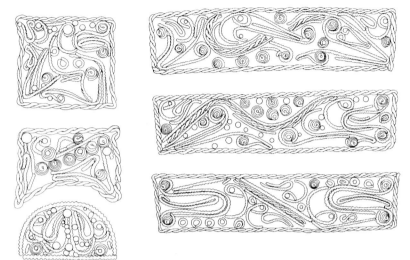

Fig 8 Details of filigree from the handle of the Derrynaflan Chalice, showing a backward-looking beast with a bird head (top), a backward-looking wingless griffin (centre) and two bird heads on a common body with touching beaks (bottom). (Drawing by Ursula Mattenberger, NMI)

Fig 9 Details from the bowl-girdle of the Derrynaflan Chalice – a beast biting its own body with two bird heads (top), a bounding quadruped, probably a lion, with bird head (centre) and a pair of beast heads with bird heads (bottom). (Drawing by Ursula Mattenberger, NMI)

amazing effect in combinations of twisted and imitation plaited wire with gold granules to emphasise detail. On some of the sides of the glass studs, knitted silver and copper wire mesh or gold filigree provides further enrichment. Stamped foils, malachite, tiny quantities of amber and a large polished rock crystal (in the centre of the underside) are used to great effect. There is no doubt that it represents a high point in the style of fine metalworking in Ireland approached by few other objects.

The smaller chalices

Although very much smaller – it is 7.6cm high and 6.5cm in diameter – the Lough Kinale chalice is remarkably similar to the larger vessels. Like the Ardagh Chalice, it has an applied lip. Its structure – it is held together by means of a pin, which passes through the cup, stem and base – follows the pattern of the other chalices. Its domed foot also recalls those of the Ardagh and Derrynaflan Chalices. It closely resembles a chalice found in a hoard concealed at Trewhiddle in Cornwall in the later ninth century.

The small bronze chalice from the Ardagh hoard and the vessel from the River Bann are very simple when compared with the large silver chalices. The Ardagh bronze vessel has a hollow trumpet-shaped foot while the River Bann Cup is provided with a solid, cast stem with a central bulbous swelling or knop. It has been suggested that such small bronze chalices were used by the celebrant while the larger

vessels were *calices ministeriales* for administering the communion wine to the faithful.

Comparison with contemporary European chalices

The Irish chalices are unusual. In Europe at the time a fashion for more slender chalices with half-egg-shaped cups and funnel-shaped feet – for example the famous Tassilo Chalice in Kremsmünster, Austria – seems to have predominated. The continental chalices employ simpler and probably sounder methods of construction. Very few European chalices have broad bowls and decorative bands, though one exception is the Gauzelin Chalice in Nancy.

A series of sixth-century Byzantine silver chalices from Syria provides some comparisons for the large bowls of the Irish vessels. One now in the Museum of Fine Arts, Boston, has a pair of handles, an inscription and, on the bowl, the monogram of Christ – the chi rho (a symbol derived from the first two letters of his name in Greek)

– in raised gilded work in the same positions as the medallions on the Ardagh Chalice. The eastern chalices survive because they were concealed in the early seventh century and thus a large number of vessels manufactured at about the same time were preserved.

Another series of Byzantine chalices made of semi-precious stone is preserved in the Treasury of St Mark's Basilica in Venice. The group includes vessels with handles, jewelled metal binding strips and other structural features that recall the decorative scheme of the Ardagh and Derrynaflan chalices. They are, however, later than the surviving Irish chalices and were mostly seized as booty in Byzantium during the Fourth Crusade.

Fig 11 The gold and jewelled chalice of Bishop Gauzelin, 13.2cm high, mid-10th century, Nancy Cathedral Treasury. (Drawing by R. Murphy, NMI)

Chalices and patens are ultimately derived from Roman tableware. As only a few medieval examples survive, resemblances between those widely separated in time and space are as likely to be traceable back to a common origin as to direct connections. Christianity had many places of pilgrimage. Of these, Rome was the most important in the west, and its basilicas were endowed with treasures from all over the Christian world. It could, therefore, have acted as a great clearing house of ideas and artistic influences and thus the Irish chalices provide no reliable evidence for the strong and direct eastern influence in Irish Christianity often canvassed.

Ornament of the chalices

The native contribution to the decoration of the chalices is obvious. Most of the ornament consists of animal and bird motifs, especially in filigree, but also engraved on the Ardagh Chalice and cast on the Derrynaflan vessel. Some of these patterns

Fig 12 Motif of two winged griffins flanking a vase on the 7th-century sarcophagus of Charenton-du-Cher, France. Behind the griffins are small trees, within which doves roost. (Drawing by C. Ryan)

37

had been borrowed by the Irish from Germanic animal styles during the seventh century and may originally have had a pagan, or at least secular, significance. By the eighth century in Ireland they may have lost all but their ornamental value, or they may have been re-assigned a Christian symbolic significance. Some are undoubtedly common Christian symbols.

The artist of the Derrynaflan Chalice had the quirk of putting bird heads in panels with beasts, and these are references to the Christian Tree of Life motif. The tree was often shown with beasts on either side (a reference to the prophecy that the Redeemer would be known between two living things) and with birds roosting in its branches. A panel on the handle of the chalice showing a pair of stylised birds with touching beaks may also be a rendering of the same design – the tree is often flanked by a pair of birds in early Christian carvings.

The Derrynaflan filigree also carries numerous depictions of the griffin – the eagle-headed lion – a beast greatly used in Christian symbolism and one which neatly reflects the two natures of Christ, who was often symbolised by the lion and the eagle separately. The filigree of the Ardagh Chalice depicts beasts, birds and serpents and may recall the varieties of living things enumerated in the Book of Genesis. We cannot assume that the artists were blindly repeating meaningless decorative themes – the Christian symbolic content may be difficult to detect, but careful observation reveals it.

The Derrynaflan Paten

The paten or communion plate from Derrynaflan is of a type which is unfamiliar to modern eyes. It measures 35.6–36.8cm in diameter and is heavily decorated. Clearly, it was not made to stand on a chalice as modern patens and many medieval ones do, but on the footed stand provided for it.

The construction of the Derrynaflan Paten is very elaborate, consisting of over three hundred separate components. It is a beaten shallow silver dish stitched with wire and soldered to a bronze rim. It was spun on a lathe to polish it. The upper surface of the edge of the dish carries twelve ornamental, gilt-bronze frames in each of which are two gold filigree panels. The side of the rim bears stamped ornamental gold foils – twelve in all – and twelve elaborate rectangular polychrome glass studs. The upper surface originally carried twenty-four elaborate and beautiful round glass studs. One of these is missing and has been replaced by a modern substitute. Twelve of the studs are large and purely ornamental. There were also originally twelve smaller studs, one of which is now lost and has been replaced by a modern reconstruction. The smaller ones are functional: they conceal the upper ends of the pins which hold the elaborate assembly together.

Fig 14 Analytical drawings of filigree panels on the Derrynaflan Paten, showing the stag with snake and the eagle with snake-headed interlace, probably a variant of the ancient motif of the eagle devouring the snake. See detail photos 15, 16. (Drawing by Ursula Mattenberger, NMI)

A hoop of silver (the stand) was associated with the paten. It clearly mimics the side of the paten in design – it carries eight die-stamped silver plates and seven, originally eight, polychrome glass studs. It is of less accomplished workmanship, however, and when the paten is placed on it the two objects are seen to clash unpleasingly. It is possible that the stand had at one time been riveted as a foot-ring to the underside of the paten. It was damaged, perhaps by being torn off the paten, in ancient times.

It is quite clear that the Derrynaflan Paten dates to about the same period as the Ardagh Chalice – indeed so close are some of the technical and stylistic resemblances especially in filigree, knitted wire mesh and glass – that the two pieces must have come from closely-related workshops.

*Photo 15
Derrynaflan
Paten, filigree
detail depicting
an eagle with
serpent-headed
interlace.
(NMI)*

*Photo 16
Derrynaflan
Paten, filigree
detail showing a
stag and serpent.
(See analytical
drawings Fig 14)*

40

*Photo 17
Derrynaflan
Paten, filigree
detail showing a
backward-looking
stag in a field
of interlace.
(NMI)*

*Photo 18
Derrynaflan
Paten, filigree
detail showing
kneeling men with
interlaced hair
and beards.
(NMI)*

Ornament of the Derrynaflan Paten

The filigree ornament of the paten consists of animal patterns, snakes, an eagle, manikins and abstract designs. Many of these may be purely ornamental but some undoubtedly had a religious connotation. The eagle, for example, could be the evangelist's symbol or could represent Christ, while a scene of a stag with snakes was taken from the ancient Bestiary – a work, originally about natural history but, in early medieval Europe, a great source of Christian allegory.

Another panel carries a single stag – a motif with strong baptismal symbolism because of the Psalmist's reference to the stag thirsting for the waters of streams.

Some interlaced ornament is arranged so that a cross pattern is shown. A complex assembly code of letters engraved on the concealed surface of many of the principal components indicates that a literate person, almost certainly a cleric, participated in its design. This must surely have been in an important church workshop. It is likely that the symbolic references in the ornament would have been understood and keenly appreciated by those who handled the paten.

As chalices derived from the drinking cups of the late Roman world, so patens originated in the plates used at table. No surviving ancient paten so distinctly recalls the Roman practice of embellishing the rims of great silver plates with scenes of beasts and men as that from Derrynaflan. Documentary sources show that such plates, originally secular, were preserved in early western church treasuries where Irish churchmen travelling on the continent could have seen them.

Comparison with other European patens

There are some very large patens from sixth-century Byzantine hoards from Syria and Turkey, some of which measure over 60cm in diameter. Although they reflect an early tradition of communion plates of very large size, they are not especially good comparisons for the Derrynaflan plate.

Later jewelled and footed patens carved from semi-precious stone, also brought from Byzantium and now in the treasury of St Mark's in Venice, demonstrate that communion plates of this type were once more widespread. Some examples are of about the same order of size as the Derrynaflan Paten. They date to the tenth and eleventh centuries AD. We know from historical sources that very large patens were once fairly common in the great western churches.

The Lough Kinale Paten

The small paten found with the Lough Kinale Chalice is in fragmentary condition. It may be reconstructed as a shallow, copper-alloy plate, tinned or gilded and about 10cm in diameter. It stood on a small domed foot of closely similar pattern to that of the chalice. It was spun on a lathe and incised lines are engraved on its upper surface.

Fig 15 Detail of an 11th-century Byzantine relief in the British Museum depicting an eagle and serpent. The motif probably represents Christ overcoming Satan. It is rare in western Christianity before the 12th century. (Drawing by C. Ryan)

The Derrynaflan Strainer

One of the objects in the Derrynaflan hoard is a strainer consisting of a bronze ladle almost 38cm long with a deep bowl, 11.5cm in diameter, and a jewelled handle-terminal equipped with a bronze ring for suspension. The rim of the bowl is decorated with stamped silver plates and glass. The bowl is divided by a strainer-plate pierced decoratively. Its rim also bears stamped foil and a glass stud.

It is not a pour-through strainer like the modern kitchen sieve. Wine was poured into one side of the bowl and flowed through the sieve plate and out the other side.

Strainers were an important part of the altar service in early times. In the eighth century in Rome two sieves were used, a larger when filling the chalice for Mass and a smaller to take from the chalice the particles of consecrated bread dropped into it at the consecration. Small liturgical sieves occur in secular Roman hoards and Byzantine church treasures from Syria and elsewhere. The Derrynaflan strainer is, therefore, the attempt of an Irish craftsman, using local ideas of design, to produce what was once an essential piece of equipment for the service of Mass.

The Derrynaflan basin may have been used in the ablutions so important in the liturgy but we cannot be certain about this.

CONCLUSION

We are fortunate that we can reconstruct an almost complete Irish altar service of the eighth to ninth centuries AD. The communion vessels tell us a great deal about the society that produced them. The materials of which they are made appear to indicate overseas trade: the amber certainly had to be imported and we know of no evidence that native sources of gold or silver were exploited at this period. Mercury used in the gilding process was imported.

The methods of manufacture used on the chalices and the Derrynaflan Paten tell us about the technology of the time; for example the lathe was used in polishing the bowls, filigree was soldered in place and a variety of hand tools were used.

Above all, however, they show that there were patrons wealthy enough to support craftsmen of great talent and that there was an audience sophisticated enough to appreciate their work. Who were these patrons and what inspired them to commission these beautiful altar vessels in the later eighth and ninth centuries? We know from later sources in Ireland and from common historical evidence elsewhere that great religious art was often commissioned by a collaboration of leading churchmen and secular rulers. This is explicitly stated in the inscriptions on some of the high crosses and reliquaries of the ninth century and later. Kings vied with one another in competitive donations to the church. For pieces such as the Ardagh and Derrynaflan treasures some such partnership of powerful lay dignitaries and churchmen is very likely, but we have no way of proving this.

The Ardagh Chalice is of unsound construction and probably never was waterproof. The decorative rims of the Derrynaflan Paten are made of wire that would have trapped particles of the communion bread. Their use would thus have jeopardised the elements of the Eucharist, respect for which was fundamental, and so there is a case for believing that they were votive objects rather than intended for actual liturgical use. The Derrynaflan Chalice, however, could have been used although it suffered so little wear and tear before it was buried that it must have been reserved for special occasions. The bronze chalices may have been for everyday use. The chalice and its paten from Lough Kinale are small enough to have been a travelling communion set.

Whether used or not, the finest Irish vessels would have been suitable for a great metropolitan church. It is easy to imagine leading Irish clerics in the eighth and ninth centuries adopting the increasingly ornate Roman liturgy of which they were fully aware and in which many of them had participated in Gaul, England and in Rome itself. It may very well be that this liturgy is embodied in monuments on the great Irish ecclesiastical sites.

Some of these had a number of churches rather than a single great one. In Rome, the pontiff celebrated Mass at different basilicas and churches on Sundays and feast days, going in solemn procession to the 'station' for the day. Bishops in other western cities copied this practice. Some early Irish ecclesiastical sites may well have been conceived of as models of the Holy City and may even have been redesigned to accommodate elaborate Roman liturgies. (The lay-out of Clonmacnoise was remodelled in the early tenth century.) In a land without cities, the monasteries would have provided the only appropriate venue for a sophisticated episcopal liturgy, and this imitation of Rome is probably the context for which the great Irish sacred vessels were created.

FURTHER READING

Henry, F. 1965 *Irish art in the Early Christian Period to AD 800*, Methuen, London

Henry, F. 1967 *Irish art during the Viking invasions, AD 800–1020*,
   Methuen, London

Manning, Conleth 1995 *Early Irish Monasteries*, Country House, Dublin

Ó Floinn, R. 1997 'The object known as the "Mias Tighearnáin"', in M. Ryan (ed.)
   Irish Antiquities, Wordwell, Dublin, 151–72

Ó Floinn, R. 1995 'Clonmacnoise: art and patronage in the Early Medieval Period',
   in C. Bourke (ed.) *From the Isles of the North: early medieval art in Ireland and
   Britain*, HMSO, Belfast, 251–60

Ryan, M. (ed.) 1983 *Treasures of Ireland*, Royal Irish Academy, Dublin

Ryan, M. 1990 'The formal relationships of insular Early Medieval eucharistic
   chalices', *Proceedings of the Royal Irish Academy*, 281–356

Ryan, M. 1998 'The Derrynaflan Hoard and early Irish art', *Speculum 72,* October
   1997, 995–1017

Youngs, Susan (ed.) 1989 *The work of angels*, British Museum Press, 1989

46

OTHER TITLES IN THE SERIES:

*Published by Country House in association with the National Museum of Ireland